Best Poems of 1971

Best Poems of 1971
Borestone Mountain Poetry Awards 1972

A Compilation of Original Poetry
Published in Magazines of the
English-Speaking World in 1971

Twenty-fourth Annual Issue
Volume XXIV

Pacific Books, Publishers, Palo Alto, California

1972

International Standard Book Number 0-87015-200-9.
Library of Congress Catalog Card Number 49-49262.
Printed and bound in the United States of America.

PACIFIC BOOKS, PUBLISHERS
P.O. Box 558, Palo Alto, California 94302

FOREWORD

Best Poems of 1971 presents the Borestone Mountain Poetry Awards of 1972, and is a selection of poems first published in magazines of the English-speaking world in 1971. The magazines and issues from which the selections were made are listed in the "Contents." By the time the compilation is completed in early 1972, some of the selections have been reprinted in book form. These subsequent reprintings and other recognitions are recorded under "Acknowledgments and Notes."

This is the twenty-fourth consecutive annual volume of selections of Borestone Mountain Poetry Awards beginning with the first issue in 1949. There have been two variations in titles since the first volume, *Poetry Awards 1949*. The fifth volume included the full name of the literary trust, *Borestone Mountain Poetry Awards 1953*, to avoid confusion with other "awards." The eighth volume identified the year of the selections, *Best Poems of 1955*, with the subtitle *Borestone Mountain Poetry Awards 1956*, which continued the sequence of earlier titles.

The few requirements established for the first volume have never been changed. A poem is eligible if it is the first printing and not over one hundred lines. Translations, unpublished poems, and reprints from other publications and books are not considered.

The editorial procedure has also been consistent throughout the twenty-four volumes. Some three hundred or more poems are selected by the reading staff each year. When the year's selections are complete, copies of the poems are sent to the judges with the names of the authors and periodicals deleted, as there is no intention of recognizing established names in preference to newcomers, or distributing selections between periodicals and countries. The judges score their individual preferences and forward the results to the office of the Managing Editor, where a tabulation of the scores determines the final selections. The three highest scores are the winners of the year's awards. Thus, there can be more than one poem by the same poet and a number of poems entered from the same periodical.

"Requiem for Sonora" by Richard Shelton received the first award of $300. "Peter's Complaint" by Van K. Brock won the second award of $200, and "Snails" by R. M. Rehder received the third award of $100.

The editors gratefully acknowledge permission to reprint these selected poems from the magazines, publishers, and authors owning the copyrights.

THE EDITORS

LIONEL STEVENSON
Chairman
HOWARD SERGEANT
British Commonwealth
Magazines
(*except Canada*)

HILDEGARDE FLANNER
FRANCES MINTURN HOWARD
GEMMA D'AURIA
WADDELL AUSTIN
Managing Editor

ACKNOWLEDGMENTS AND NOTES

"Requiem for Sonora" by Richard Shelton, selected from the original printing in the September 4, 1971 issue of *The New Yorker*, appears in his chapbook, *Calendar*, published in May 1972 by Baleen Press, Phoenix, Arizona. The poem will be included in his next book, *Of All the Dirty Words*, to be published by University of Pittsburgh Press in October 1972.

"Flies" by Lloyd Abbey also has appeared in *The Antlered Boy*, a collection of poems by Lloyd Abbey and John Ferns, published by the University of New Brunswick.

"Roadside Notes in Ragged Hand Driving from South Carolina" by James Applewhite, copyright © 1971 by Minneapolis Star and Tribune Co., Inc., is reprinted from the September 1971 issue of *Harper's Magazine* by permission of the author.

"Zero," copyright © 1971 by Wendell Berry, was selected from the first publication in *The Hudson Review*, Vol. XXIV, No. 2, Summer 1971, and is also from his forthcoming volume, *The Country of Marriage*, to be published by Harcourt Brace Jovanovich, Inc.

"A Son Returns," copyright © by Sam Bradley, was selected from the Winter 1971 issue of *Southwest Review*, and will be included in his next book, *manspell/godspell*, to be published by Anvil Press Poetry, London, England.

"New thoughts on 'A Song on the End of the World'" by Martin Booth is from the first printing in *Outposts* and has subsequently appeared in his book, *The Crying Embers*, published by Fuller d'Arch Smith, Ltd., London, England.

"Invocation, an Elegy" by Jerald Bullis is from the Winter 1970 issue of *The Yale Review*, copyright © Yale University, and will be included in his next book, *Taking Up the Serpent*, to be published by Ithaca House, Ithaca, New York.

"A House: For Shirley" by William Dickey is also from his book, *More Under Saturn*, copyright © 1971 by William Dickey, which was published by Wesleyan University Press.

Two poems, "The Snapper" and "The Swan," by William Heyen first appeared in *Poetry*, copyright © 1971 by The Modern Poetry Association, and are reprinted by permission of the Editor of *Poetry*. "Texts" by William Heyen is from *The Western Hu-*

CONTENTS

REQUIEM FOR SONORA

1

a small child of a wind
stumbles toward me down the arroyo
lost and carrying no light
tearing its sleeves
on thorns of the palo verde
talking to itself
and to the dark shapes it touches
searching for what it has not lost
and will never find
searching
and lonelier
than even I can imagine

the moon sleeps
with her head on the buttocks of a young hill
and you lie before me
under moonlight as if under water
oh my desert
the coolness of your face

2

men are coming inland to you
soon they will make you the last resort
for tourists who have
nowhere else to go

what will become of the coyote
with eyes of topaz
moving silently to his undoing
the ocotillo
flagellant of the wind
the deer climbing with dignity
further into the mountains
the huge and delicate saguaro

what will become of those who cannot learn
the terrible knowledge of cities

3

years ago I came to you as a stranger
and have never been worthy
to be called your lover or to speak your name
loveliest
most silent sanctuary
more fragile than forests
more beautiful than water

I am older and uglier
and full of the knowledge
that I do not belong to beauty
and beauty does not belong to me
I have learned to accept
whatever men choose to give me
or whatever they choose to withhold
but oh my desert
yours is the only death I cannot bear

RICHARD SHELTON

PETER'S COMPLAINT

1

After supper, we argued over stars
While you went off, saying, "Keep watch for soldiers."
But supper was too heavy and we slept.

You woke us with such quiet admonishment
That, seeing the flares, I was whelmed with guilt
And would have killed a fellow with my knife
Had you not stopped me, saying, "I'll go," and gone
To show us what your words had always meant.

But seeing word as fact, I felt betrayed
And said, "I never knew him in my life."

2

Hidden in my mantle, in the mob,
Planning to purge my flesh of a sick dream,
I watched you hung, outstretched, above our heads.

The sun grew black in eclipse, ringed thin with light,
Then was itself again, so suddenly
That those who watched grew blind. Terror had turned
My dark eyes inward. It was then you died.

3

Since we had met in groves often at night,
I found it harder now to reconcile
Your sunburned flesh, your new, translucent face.

Yet having to wear a beard taught compromise:
I! Me! a native of the oath.
Egyptian, Persian, Greek and Roman—we
Saw all powers turning on one spit,
The light and dark, flesh, mind and spirit.

They hung me upside down. The nails were keys
To kingdoms—the empire, then its conquerors.

4

Authority had so fixed our eyes on quiet
Atriums that we, inured to nature now,
Judged all landscapes by our secluded gardens.
Triumphant, we became the absolute,
Bent men to God, burned books, castrated statues,
Structured time, foreshadowed revolutions.

Cathedrals of stressed logic, bound and buttressed
By new hierarchic heraldry, told our story.
The Word, woven into stone-dark facades
That anchored tall shafts spanned with colored glass,
Held up our stone tents, pitched high in the air.

Spirit infused matter, *mater omnium,*
Chanted new quantums, through stained and filtered dark,
While under drowsing lids we worshipped light.

5

Mist in a wind, the light of ancience, distilled,
Began to rain and freshen stagnant water.
When everything withers into the new year,
While winter holds time frozen in its mind,
We do not know what new thoughts spring will have.

The stars have grown too great to comprehend,
Too far (or near) to argue, and turned from silver
To flame. The blood runs upward toward the brain.
Our minds grow younger while our hearts grow old.

But God inhabits, while eluding, all ideas
And will be found again in wind and waves,
Subject, like us, to fortune and to rumor.

The churches crowd the planet of hunger. Children
Make crosses of sticks and wish for food—
Awed at your monuments, museums of torture
Devices: the cross itself, edicts against
Prevention and abortion, the anomalies of birth,
Pickled grotesqueries.

Crosses orbit. Cathedrals spin toward the moon.

6

I try to remember if you are what we remembered,
But cannot clearly remember you—
And never saw you clearly. When we both were,
The air was always filled with vapors of dawn,
The dust of day, the haze of twilight, starlight.
Our sight was never steady or finely shaded.
And I was not a rock. It surprises me
They say you said so. What I was is vague
Even to me. For I have been confused
With fact and legend since that old impermanence.
Even as I speak I am being altered.

7

Though we have been hard grains in the sieve,
We dissolve in streams, disperse, and strained by earth,
Are assumed again by time, crossed with dream.
On the rack constellations of the night,
The motion of the wheel grinds and scatters in space
Until we rain out of abyss itself.

But the heart's savage mob forcing our door
Is crying for blood, the old sacrament,
Though we have turned, like all magic, to myth.
Thus they are turning from us and we from them.
Yet we are shackled, ourselves a cross, to stars
That twist us as they turn and turn and turn.

VAN K. BROCK

SNAILS

Snails are—like long journeys—
Occasions for meditation,
For thinking which is neither
The forming of problems
Or the choosing of solutions,
Nor reminiscence,
Nor even the imposition of patterns,
But that continuous metamorphosis
Which is the mind's carding and churning,
As when a spectator in an old amphitheater
Dreams beyond the action
Or looks out of the theater.

They are the great pedestrians,
Moulds of instinct,
Vauban's rivals,
Complete as the open rose.
Private, solitary and exemplary,
Companions of our exile,
They teach, by their simplicity,
The building of form:
The recourse of complication and symmetry.
I compare their superior terseness
To the magistral honeycomb;
Yet they are closer to Chartres and unfinished Beauvais
Than to those gardens the Japanese admire
Which are only smooth stones in smooth sand.

They, who love surfaces,
Are turned by the mind
In the same way the mind
Adheres to its own troubles.
Everpresent consciousness is a heavy shell
With its own involvements.

Approaching happiness
I anticipate its sweetness
And figure in advance
Its final shape,
The hardening which is loss,
Casting the moment before it happens,
Feeling only my own structure
Like a snail in its shell.

The snail embodies
My dialogue with myself,
Hidden sensitivity,
Where anyone who looks can see
Loneliness within loneliness
And all the torments of lucidity.

R. M. REHDER

FLIES

Pacing upon the chandelier,
she moves like Mrs. Jesus—
a six-legged beauty,
striding the ballroom floor.
In the glass she sees
her two jewelled eyes,
as intricate as honeycombs,
then, modestly,
a leg covers her head.
For a male has discerned
her onyx gaze,
the hair that bristles her thorax,
her quivering tongue,
electric as a snake's.
He buzzes his approval
and stridently they reconstruct
the twelve-legged fly,
his tongue tattooing her forehead.
Great will be their progeny,
the swarmers of schoolroom windows,
the offal-scavengers,
paper-dodgers,
jewellers of garbage piles.
Their maggots in the butter block
shall make it walk like Lazarus.
Their glory shall be magnified
in heads of green and gold.

And though he, victim of cruel boys,
will horribly lose his members,
she, carrying new disease,
will end a line of potentates
who never once
bowed down
to lord or thunder.

LLOYD ABBEY

ALL THE PRETTY ONES

Sometimes I wish he would enter,
the whispering salesman who would sell
me eternity. I wish he would come here
with the usual, saucy, red carnation
in his buttonhole, stagily bowing,
his words badly dubbed into English,
not quite synchronizing with his lips.

But I know he does not exist.
I am not easily spoofed. Right now, though,
(1 A.M.) I expect some wild-eyed character
near a tombstone in Highgate cemetery
is trying to chant him up
with this or that spell,
some ancient, clapped-out ceremony.

I'm a rational man, touch wood,
yet if that glib whisperer existed,
if he came here now with a hey presto,
a magnesium flash and a silly puff of smoke,
I bet he'd be carrying a Kensitas silver tray
on which, next to the silver tongs, a glass
of soap bubbles would be boiling over.

They would rise into the air.
They would float deliciously, they would sail
in their transparencies of cathedral silence,
and soon, very soon, he would be gloating,
"All the pretty ones, all the pretty ones,"
as the bubbles burst on soundless objects,
on the walls, on the indifferent ceiling.

You would never catch me after dark
in Highgate cemetery, but if he came here
(he does not exist) I would haggle,
I would trade my absolute desolations
of "no" and "no" for one ephemeral "maybe,"
that a single coloured bubble might not burst,
that a door might open for its triumphant exit.

DANNIE ABSE

THESE TREES

The houses there
where nothing is thrown out
have lawns and gardens
and weigh very much:

they are sinking with their weight
into the earth,
the trees around them
get higher, thicken,
and children climb
toward lightness.

Crawling along the branches,
the heedless children
are pulled down
into the leaves
as into whirlpools:

waving arms
while the green floods over them,
they are carried off,
whirled away.

On the other side
of the leaf is
a room
entirely composed
of furniture:

chair next to chair
going around a table,
a table in the center, on the sides
sideboards blocking the walls,
and chairs in the corners

with small tables beside them
—a room which sits upon planks

and waits, tense, with such strain,
the colors drain out,
it grows white—
then,

now one, now
one other rap
inside a tabletop, a
creak in a chair leg, creaks
like sobs, and tappings
in the wood, moan in floorboards:

the children
are crawling inside the furniture,
looking for cracks
to squeeze through
before they drown:
their fingers run
every which way, their fists
try to beat a way out.

The noises subside,
tap by slow tap:
no one has left,
they are all drowned,
all in the wood,
still in the wood,

and the room is so white, so still,
it almost loses its substance
to become a condition of the air
like oppressive weather.

JACK ANDERSON

AN OWL

"the necessary angel," Wallace Stevens

When you are aware of more than you can see,
an owl hunts a hedgerow at evening.

And it is only on the point of evaporation
that you glimpse it,
that a blob of congealed dusk becomes visible,
a little darker than white, a little heavier,
a little more positive
than the mist over the fields
                        this gathered softness
tilts, lifts, brushes the silence behind the eyes

and crossing from one sodden field to another sodden field
disappears over the roof of the car
to shake out elsewhere
the long undulating scarf of its cry.

It is the angel of its own annunciation,
the announced angel
sucked back as soon as seen
down the baroque perspective of departure

and you know it already, know it deeply,
although you have barely caught
the floating freckled shadow of your belief.

So Mary must have known
the faint fastidious presence
when the angel offered the incarnate image
hunter of hedgerows, most difficult of sons
who as he stooped ascended into absence.

PATRICK ANDERSON

ROADSIDE NOTES IN RAGGED HAND
DRIVING FROM SOUTH CAROLINA

Meeting her has torn me open to feel everything again

oak leaves broken to fists by winter, still clinging branches,
    that crunch into my feelings like pebbles
I have in my chest the hidden water running like song
  birds quick-hidden where the brush piles:
                        berries on a spray
I think of my wife without guilt
                yet landscape of so many emotions
yet wear of the time and distance between us
my flesh hill-edge clay rusting to gullies.

Plenty of buzzards this blue day
    balancing on windy edges the clouds make
four wooden cows far on a hillslope
            as if a very small hand had set them there

buzzards tentative and rocking
    handling with upbent feathers at wingtip edges
currents bulking up into sky
big as water tank towering pines, boulders to fat
the clouds irregular cheeks
               it is love I think
which likens these four things together
        the bird the cloud the tree the stone
without it rivers would not run
        and all things break apart to dissimilitude.

Halfway home I remember first love with my wife
    all dark gullies with grass in any country
remind me of then, deep cave
trickled shining and keen with a skein
which fates my wandering always
            engaging manhood

now as I approach home broomstraw is roseate, moving
satiate with winter light on all fields around me
     the last stretch of road I take is dirt
clay trail red as flesh, cobbled with many rocks like buds of a tongue.

JAMES APPLEWHITE

THE MAN WHO MADE ME LATE FOR WORK

It happened at five minutes to eight on Monday morning.
In the grim dawn of a new work-week I drove slowly,
stubborn and unyielding as a cod in a school of mullet.
Andretti-inflamed clerks in clerky cars swarmed by;
stenos in tiny cars sculpted their hair en route;
downtown merchants, in wine or neon-yellow shirts,
guided heavy dark sedans like flagships of commerce
and assayed the profit-weather with trained sniffs.

Then, at our key intersection, traffic stopped dead.
In seconds, cars backed up a block all ways.
Because there, starting a diagonal crossing
in flaunt of local ordinance, golden and glorified
in a swath of early sun cutting past the buildings,
was surely the world's oldest, most misshapen man.
Drivers too far back to see honked and ranted,
but we in the front ranks were silent in wonder.
I felt stunned. Nothing staged could duplicate this
living, forming masterpiece, a song for the eyes.
He was Man the majestic, the unflinching and unbreakable.

Could any creature be so slow? Any rockbound root as bent?
His frail shoes did not rise a full inch at a step.
His feet did not land; they kissed. Yet, he soared.
An immense old Army pack, the color of swamps,
humped sharp as a butte over his caved shoulders
like the sacked burdens of ten lifetimes.
But he came on. My God, what a marvel to see him loom
through that light: part crab, part goat and granite
                                        and angel.

He did not look up. Perhaps deaf to the circling city,
certainly unaware of being the crux of a tableau,
he held track, pecking ahead with a twisted walking stick,
white hair and beard like frozen spray on a ship's prow.

Three cycles of the lights were needed for his traverse
and no car cut his wake until he gained the curb.
Safe atop the sidewalk slab, he paused to shift his pack.
With one brown hand on a signal standard, the old man bobbed
like an ouzel on a river rock. As he eased his load
the spell ended. The blessed became the ordinary;
the traffic roiled.

I turned the corner without a glance, unwilling
to see what I guessed his real face might be.
But I was the one revealed false and unlovable,
in thinking: with all the winds to greet his dying dance,
with brother hawks to share his final flight on earth,
what difference would it make if I had stopped to say
Good morning, Sir?

FREDERICK BENTON

ZERO

The river streams in the cold.
Above it the streams
impend, locked like iron
in the frozen hollows. The cold
reaches of the sky
have leapt onto the ground.
But the wren's at home
in the cubic acre of his song.
House and shed and barn
stand up around their lives
like songs. And I
have a persistent music in me,
like water flowing under ice,
that says the warmer days
will come, blossom and leaf
return again. I live in that,
a flimsy enclosure,
but the song's for singing
not to dread the end.
The end, anyhow, is always here.
It is the climate we sing in.
A man may ease off into it
any time, like a settler,
tired of farming, starting out
silently into the woods.
On a day like this we have
the end in sight. This is zero,
the elemental poverty
of all that was ever born,
in which nothing lives by chance
but only by choosing to
and by knowing how—and by
the excess of desire that rises
above the mind, surrounding
and hovering like a song.

WENDELL BERRY

NEW THOUGHTS ON "A SONG ON THE END OF THE WORLD"

Czesław Miłosz

The night the world forecloses
will not be filled with a thrushing
                sound of moths
nor the rabid whispers of fire

there will be no happy porpoises
no wild laughter
no randy drunk sailors
no animated birds no glimmering
                sea

only
there will be an awareness
a silence a peace
as quiet as a stillbirth

awed noise will hold its breath
wind will stand stock-still
air will be amazed
it has no more function

air will be a prophet shaping
                its empty whimpers
into thoughts

air will be a mother of invention
it will discover invent create in
                its stillness

air will remember
trees it shook flowers it procreated
birds that used it the moon that
                rose through its frozen
depth

the night the world stops
will be a quick easily-lost moment
when creation pauses

it will be a time when never becomes a truth
it will be a time when music is muffled

the foreclosing of the world
will bring a silence that is itself
a symphony

MARTIN BOOTH

✳ A SON RETURNS

After seeing the fishlike sculpture, "Prodigal Son," by Cosmo Campoli

A threshold prodigal, thriftless,
    I come from the thriving sea.
        Prey-master, as well as favored bait,
    I dragged to conscious limits, an idolatry
        of limits. Land fool,
    I was here before the Christian toe
        fished the dust.
            Ocean cast in foam
        my pride and fate.
    "Fish! Fish!" my old flesh-hunting father
    shook the cape with shocks of woe.
            Settled forms stayed home.

        Vaingold, the family name.
    I have had Lilith and the daughters of Lilith;
        they close doors by which I came.
    Now, with surf's fertility, I spume,
        regress, acknowledge and impede
            fattened zeroes.
        Cold eyes of Kraken feed
            on a procession from nadir.
            Remembered shores erode.
    The Fisherman asks, "What is this
            tidething, wildcome,
            this wet hunger for dust?"

        Measured human by bloodtrust,
    I want back, old father. I return,
        and lo, each eye's a wide
            round of definition.
    I have cooled my cauldron breath.
    Where tidal multitudes divide
        living waters, I
    pass through the dying, the dead, the death.

Do not favor phantoms from whom I flee,
   but hear my high surf-cry.
I come against limits, I command a white road.

Now let the measuring earth know me.

SAM BRADLEY

INVOCATION, AN ELEGY

All I have of Doc Gaye, who set my poisoned right
Foot right, is a cross-cut scar he gave me when I
Was fourteen. But he begins to come more and more
True, bleach-eyed and somehow sinuous, with time
And luck. Now, if I think of a gutshot buck
Bedding down in its last night on earth, or of
A car-torn coon stretched moon-stricken, kicking,
Where the dead sicken with the taste of mine dust
In the burnt-out south of Missouri, it is only to find
Him once more in the eye

Of a boy falling, fallen into fang-driven sleep.
It is to make him come clear, here, at least,
As that lonely-living partaker of private fury
Who mysteriously lost his wife many years before
I found the wrong path in an orchard, and began to walk
With more than I'd bargained for. Gone perhaps
Are the rent limbs of soldiers he patched and tucked
In place, as a surgeon in two world wars: gone
As the eloquent fog of rye, in my memory,
That was upon his breath:

(Or the field where I tunnelled through honeysuckle
Near the still roil of a greensnake
Among still blossoms, in an aura of sweetness that takes
The breath away: where I hobbled my imaginary bay
In the sure eye of the lizard, quick
In the sun, never thinking of Doctor Gaye)
—But the dowager owner of over half the town?
Will she ever forget that incurable pinch like a bite,
In this life or any other, in the drugstore next
To his office, time and again?

Watching him lurch at you on the sidewalk, he
Could be like anything you'll dream of meeting

On the wrong path; and in foul-smelling tweeds,
As pebbly-splotched as the skin of a diamondback,
Looking lithe as a sprinter, he pulled his car one day
Onto a wooded lane while making a house call,
Turned off the ignition, lay down, and died of a heart
Attack. He cut me back to life. Now I
Must go: back into cherishable lies, into the bad
Performance of my youth,—

Into the eye-bewitching chiaroscuro of timber.
I must take certain paths again, with a foot changed
Forever. I will follow old ways to God knows where
They disappear: beside a barn unused since the 'thirties,
A ramshackle outdoor privy, or a smoke-shed
Near a weathered clapboard house, where black-
berries grow in the windows of the parlor: where
In the chinks of the fireplace, the rattlesnake
Composes his fury: waiting: accursed, accumbent,
Coiled round the dark of his eyes.

JERALD BULLIS

✳ ON BEING TOLD THAT ANIMALS
LIVE IN ABSOLUTE TIME

What kind of time they live in
only they know.
On plains, perhaps, in jungle
wilderness, or where bush and thorn
nourish the wildebeest and doe.
But here in this public park
is it always for the first time
the impala leaps against the grill?
Or the panther
crawls into the matching dark?
Does the bear
rattle his iron cage
only in the Eternal Now?
And is it always new
when the leopard coughs his rage?
Without yesterday or tomorrow
there is no need of hope.
Only today—for the first time [they tell us],
the flamingo flies against the net,
the sky is roofed
above the antelope.

JEAN BURDEN

✳ GROUND

This stuff is what we are born of. Before my eyes
And between my fingers—grainy, sticky, chalky—
The conditions lie at hand for life to burst out of.
How stubbornly it behaves, baked hard as biscuits
In summer, yet, thawed by spring, spreading wide
To swallow a hundred horses, and in winter
Rigid enough to scrape knuckles and crack bones.
It would seem to yield no passage, except that roots
As delicate as hairs can pierce hardscrabble
Without a bruise or blister and hold their course
Whether opposed by gravel or mud. By tasting it
Farmers can guess at what may come of its favors,
Whether their crops will require manure or limestone.
We savor in the first-plucked leaf of lettuce
The lingering fragrance of Sun, which slips away
To the soil that bestowed it almost within the hour,
Just as fish lose their colors out of water.
Just as I would despair, if you were dead.

PETER DAVISON

A HOUSE: FOR SHIRLEY

I see it's no real use to ask for attention.

A poem is a house in the mind. I live there.
Archimedes lives there. I don't ask
you to admire him.

         But if you *should* admire him
then the house has walls hung with tapestries that show
scenes of great love, of great effort & accomplishment
and on the floors there are silk-knotted carpets
intricate with patterns of thin noble men in profile
carrying hawks, & with patterns of evasive but
promising moon-breasted women & in the sweet
warmth of the jasmine garden outside there is the
song of a nightingale who pierces his endless breast
with his endless beak for love and pain.

That is not Archimedes, you say, looking at me with misgiving.

No, but it is the idea of a house, and all houses are houses.
We *live* there.

Again, no use to ask after attention.

But look.

Here I am, drawing this simplest, only this simplest figure
    in this plain white sand.

Come inside.

WILLIAM DICKEY

GREEK ARCHAEOLOGIST

When we were students we went on field expeditions,
Digging on sites, camping at night near villages
Or sleeping rough by the seashore; sometimes talking,
Sometimes listening all night to air and water.

Sometimes we slept in barns. Were offered bread
And cheese and wine. The men came home by moonlight,
Home from the vineyards. Lay down and slept. At morning
Rinsed out their mouths and went back to the planting.

Our passion was the past towards which we laboured
On hands and knees, sifting among the ruins,
And over the past a skin of joy—the present,
That radiant landscape rolled out on the world.

Running to work we waved to our friends in the vineyards.
They eased bent backs, and then, as we had seen them
On fragments of vases, turned again to their toil,
Cleaving the rock with an axe where the new vine would be planted.

ROSEMARY DOBSON

DEATH IN THE MINES

Think of man praying. He raises his hands to God.
Whatever his doubts, he has come to this attitude.
It is a skyward and an outward penetration.
The man praying tries to penetrate mysteries which are heavy,
Which turned his hands downward to earth, its common work,
In any hope beyond the common disasters of time.

Then I read of the miners of Cape Rosier
Who, descending into the interior of the earth,
Exercised their hands upward to pick the rocks above,
As if they could uncover and pluck some ultimate stone.
Thinking not of Samson pulling down his temple,
They struck (one stroke!) one ore so rich in meaning
Devastation shook, and killed them in a pile of rubble.

They are dead, a common lot. America goes on.
The nation rides on the skin of the planet, multitudinously.
As malfunctioned astronauts might ride around the planet
Dead until they disintegrate to a cinder, a puff
Finally as light and delicate as an April daffodil,
Influential members of mysterious time,
The dead miners in the slow growth of their disintegration

Express the serious, interior reality of poetry.
Ride easy, earth, in your strong contention,
You are stronger than man, and ride us down.
But a wind will spring up, a spirit arise
And ride on the air lightly, supremely clear,
In other centuries, and in other civilizations.

RICHARD EBERHART

WORDS FOR THE YOUNG DANCER

*We are told how Miss Graham instructing the youngest students
in the* port de bras *has had them conduct the arms from* en
haut *to* en bas *in the time it takes to say 'I am _____, thank
you life,' each uttering his own name in the provided space,
and how much less hasty they are to complete the movement.*

Do not think these things undifficult child
though you see the vast galaxy of possible worlds
engraved in this jade talisman,
you must do more than think. It is not simple
sitting grounded in the dark
to look up and watch my dance fly before me,
to follow through the spotlight
an unbroomed witch flying in the moon's face.
As though if I didn't breathe for that gazelle
dancing my part, it would collapse: my heart stops short
before the leap that hurls her through the air.

Look—how the shining seed
that hovered so long in mid-air, pulsing, springs
clutching ground and clouds at once!
I have made her walk proud on the earth,
not above it, the spine a string of matched pearls
that bows without foreshortening, then exultant
spirals whipping lean arms into the vortex!
Like blood the seamless movement circulates
dancing to the heartbeat, and the heart beats back,
endless and undiminished, rising
she spins, stops, and the spin goes on.

Nothing stops, that once alive is deathless,
and we'll laugh at those who lie down at the end!
But I have witnessed the tragedies of the best
driven until they had no more to give
and swore I would not follow them. This is nothing
undifficult child. The voice sang
years within me: I am Martha, thank you life.

That has become my students' catechism (replacing
my name with their own of course) while now
I am the dances I have made
for them, and I have only death to thank.

So the fuse might blow out the stage-lights,
rosin descend and resettle, powder on the hardwood:
I could say 'I have done'   again
not pointing to a new world but moving there. . . .

DANIEL MARK EPSTEIN

CEREMONY

Lower your voice: we are passing the school for the deaf.
Raise your hand to a horrible acquaintance.
Lower your eyes: we are passing the workshop of the blind.
Raise your lips to an old whore's smile.
Lower your head: we are passing the insane asylum.
Raise your hat to the shining hearse.

So shall you enter into the mansions of the just
And dwell for a moment within the holy mountain
Of the pitiful, the ceremonious,
Who acknowledge, without accepting, all the imperfections
Whether of mind or body, only by these gestures
Which are all we have, and whose performance
Is the one ritual binding us together, the quick, the damned
    and the dead.

The ceremony of the dry martini
Is also important. Chill the glasses.
Observe the right proportion of ingredients. Stir slowly.
Strain. Pour. And then
Drink to each other with the lips
Which are also the lips of love
To be loosened in delightful discourse
Which is also the measure of a certain music,
Of the intellectual spaces and the spheres
Dividing and joining in such perfect interrelation
As make Chaos and Old Night gnash their dry disorderly
    teeth.

Despair, too, is struck down by ceremony,
Nor can pale dejection stand against it.
Madness itself is beaten down by ceremony,
That jewel not found in the earth but fashioned
Out of earth and shining from the hands that made it,
The hands of all men who equate measure with solace,
And the formal, always, with the good;

Who striving forever in the ancient flux and darkness
To establish a congruency between their atoms and their
    actions
Between the eternity of their dreams
And the doomed pulses they inherit
Simply raise and lower the flag of their hearts.

Not too long is the road before us,
This street that must be made a meadow,
This money that must be turned to beauty,
These maladies and tortures that must be driven back to
    their paternal darkness,
But not too short for a man to raise his hand
Against the evil Accuser of his world,
The everlasting tempter and adversary
Whose peace is in negation and indifference,
Whose work is done by the cool abstracted stare.

JOHN GLASSCO

ALBUM LEAF

für Elise

Michael at the piano, silent,
Son without words set to music,
Ten small years from total mystery,
Opens the keyboard's smiling moonlit meadow
Hedged with shadowy accidentals.

Life looks out attentive from his eyes,
Candid as the clear regard of mirrors.
Gathering thoughts surprise the supple wrists,
And soon the invited notes emerge;
A charming population dancing a ballet of fingers.

I recognize a seed of the now immortal nine,
One of the master's early candle-lit inventions
Called to mind before his ears died young
Enclosing heavenlier audience; who from giant loneliness
Became a glorious sun chosen by planets.

So we meet again, immaterial visitant,
Angel in the heart—music—
Sheer unceasing source invisibly arising.
My spirit also leaps in lambs of joy
Linked like an echo to your gentle calling

As from the favouring heights
Familiar pastures rise within our hearing,
Leaving a passionate roomscape magnified by sound,
Hands of a child like hovering birds
Poised over a pale silence.

Let them learn to scale the steeper harmonies
Of this most holy art in any world—
Our loving reassertion making the gift fruitful—
That this green beginning also
May grow into a summer.

ROBERT GORDON

THIS CITY NOW . . . .

Autumn hunts you down, year after year,
Nudging you first with a red flag in a morning lane
Hung out, stiff, in the mist—
Little sounds: the crunch of an apple—
Faint smells: bonfire smoke. Chrysanthemums. Dusk.
It's been padding after you ever since your first,
Your very first party, in the first dark evening
In your best frock, white socks, clean hanky,
Present for hostess heavy in your hand—excitement.
    Already, already
    Nostalgia.
Edwardian, Victorian feelings—even then,
                                    Already
Looking back. An ache. A luxury of dying. Very strange.

It'll get you, somewhere. Will it be here, under the plane trees
In The Mall? Under those clustered bobbles
    Hung . . . in the mist, in the air.
So quiet. Or in Trafalgar Square?
Where a red bus looms and is gone again,
Traffic is coming and fading; a taxi one side moves
Unknown to a taxi the other side. Blinkers on everyone.
Mystery. Who is in there? *Who is there?*
Someone is waiting, just breathing, born.
Prince Charming—is *he* at the party?

People are back at work now, after the scattered summer,
Things of importance can happen here: meetings, planning,
Ideas. Idea of a party, idea of a city.
Brisk, morning mist. A tough, resilient season,
Deliberately concealing its plans for Spring.
People have got to be deceived by the bobbles,
The dustcarts, the oceans of leaves, the echoes and yearning,
The nudgings, the isolation, the mist, the ache,
The backward tugging and drawing to Christmas, December.

(These months that keep ending in "ember"—
Such echoes. Such whispers. Such hiding in corners. Remember).
The hunting goes on, dogging your muffled footsteps.
Someone, something for you, in the mist. Exciting.

It may be here, in Malet Street, by this new building
—Empty as yet, but pleasing, with pillars and overhang,
Waiting for autumn term, young people, couples
Meeting for the first time, immemorially, round these corners,
These pillars, with vistas through—unusual in London—
To yellowing leaves, old, terraced houses,
Plane trees, and Novembers in all great cities.
(This world, this world, has it always been old?
Since its very first party, at three, or four?
A big, brass knocker on the door.
Welcome, and lights, and delight—
Your present, so very important, so mysterious,
So full of hope. You look up from the wrapping, a little child
A la recherche du temps perdu . . .)

It is best to be a new building in autumn.
You quickly become old, with piles of leaves
In all your rawest, newest angles.
These leaves have always known they would one day be old.
They meet it with such singular resignation. They seem to love it.
They accept drifts, and even dustcarts.
And the plane trees in Russell Square, they are big, and old,
                and beautiful.
"An unusual collocation of words" says a sensitive African,
Willing, but not quite able, to understand.
For the trees in his childhood, though big, and old
And no doubt beautiful also in their way
Could not know an English November. November in such a city.
Nor an English child's shiver and thrill,
Waiting for the door to open on the party—
Rustling of paper, and autumn leaves—and already
                A chill.

Already a sense of heaviness—of wanting to lie
Beneath a cover of leaves on the cold ground,
And be unwrapped, discovered at last, accepted—found.

JULIET GOWAN

A CLUTCH OF DREAMS

The forked path in the woods
Dreams of a crossroads,
A perfection in concrete, dividing
This valley into four equal fields;

The shoat at the slaughterhouse door
Remembers a fine, white gate
At the barn-end of a meadow
And corn calling with the voice of a man.

Waterlogged, the orange liferaft
Drifts on the wide-eyed Pacific
Then sinks, still dreaming of atolls,
And the new crew roistering ashore.

And I, on this forked path
Of dreams, I see fine white gates
And I ride this orange-raft world
Downward towards coral, where all dreams end.

JAMES B. HALL

A PLACE TO LIVE IN

Nothing is merciful—
not even you, Oh Lord,
whom we have mercilessly
forsaken.
The autumn underfoot
smells sweet of pine;
blue wind socks through
the hemlocks;
robins swoop in,
to swap stands in the trees.
The skies labor
with heavy planes
and piles of clouds.
Whetting a knife,
rocking a scythe,
poor man, rich thief,
dead and gone—
stone walls to silence—
yet hanging on
in us, the merciless:
because we thought,
because we acted,
because we traded in
our love
unknowingly,
because we used the living
for our lives,
burning with hope
and cruelty;
while the earth rolled over,
roaring, soothing itself,
mindless in its pain.

JOHN HAY

THE SNAPPER

He is the pond's old father, its brain
and dark, permanent presence.

He is the snapper, and smells
rich and sick as a mat of weeds; and wears

a beard of leeches that suck frog, fish,
and snake blood from his neck; and drags

a tail ridged as though hacked out
with an axe. He rises: mud swirls

and blooms, lilies bob, the water washes
his moss-humped back where, buried

deep in his sweet flesh, the pond ebbs
and flows its sure, slow heart.

WILLIAM HEYEN

THE SWAN

The sun reached pond's edge, past
lily-of-the-valley smoldering
in deep shade,

past oaks scrawled with vines
dripping the ink tears
of wild grape,

reached to the end of a path lined with thistles,
to a cove defined by cattails, to kindle
the corpse of a swan:

whose bill was a tiger lily,
whose eyes burned blind
to the rising sun.

Wind rose to lift its quills, to fan
the white flames of its wings.
Dark water floated

the swan's neck, now curved limp
as a snake's shed skin.
I breathed

the pond's pollen, studied the water's haze
where spiders and sprites walked,
bugs swam circles,

and pads curled their edges. At noon,
mud swirled and flowered,
the pond towed

the swan away: that said nothing, nothing
but the black light that flared
from its eyes as it sailed.

WILLIAM HEYEN

TEXTS

1

Twain meant that as Huck drifted
toward Jackson's Island
he was already dead.
He'd killed a pig
and splashed its blood around
and stuck his hair to an axe
for Pap to find, and later,
hiding near shore,
hidden by brush and the thick fog
of a dream, he heard, between
cannon-thumps and rushes of wind,
voices he knew from the old life,
and watched loaves of bread
weighted with quicksilver
float by to find him.
But Twain meant that by this time

Huck was already dead,
and this island, island of dream,
dark, heavy-timbered,
"like a steamboat," he says,
"like a steamboat without any lights,"
this island toward which,
already dead, Huck drifted,
this island that seemed,
like Fulton's ships on the Hudson,
to be driving up river,
is prophecy, this
is the country, this has something
to do with sadness, this
is what he saw, this
is what he knew, this
dark island is the rest of the story.

2

The beginning exists in the end,
the end in the beginning.
Huck knew what was ahead was
the machine and a love
to accept and despair of.
In the beginning,
before we lived or chose to,
the machine rose up
from the fog, the steamboat
dividing the river, and the cities
were always there
under the dark water,
and where men settled
wheat waved golden in the sun,
threshers rose up from the soil,
and all the old sins

filled the sails of ships
that first drove homeward
to America. And Twain knew,
and Dreiser, and fated Hart Crane,
and Faulkner, whose Ike watched
the two-toed bear older
than legend, the great "locomotive-
like shape," appear and disappear
like a whale in its swirl;
and Ben, the locomotive, slain,
the engine rounds the bend
of the wilderness again, where
it was born. In the beginning
and in the end, in the dream
and in the dream's end,
the land smells of metal.

WILLIAM HEYEN

DOOM

People are not much absorbed with it
These days, it is not part of existence,
Of great moment or imperative concern;
Obscurely they feel they have conquered it,
It is overshadowed by more important matters:
It cannot be reconciled with success,
Does not fit their projections, have a shape
That can be analysed, lend itself to calculations;
Cannot be made to serve them, inspire
Effort, is out of place with their comforts.

Once they thought they would know it
By a rumbling beneath the surface of the earth,
A trembling that made their limbs shudder,
A dark gulf of nothing opening before them;
They awaited a natural catastrophe, fire or ice,
A silence of deafness descended upon the world,
Pupil of the eye become a black drop of infinity.

Now those who think of it at all wonder
If their anxieties have anything to do with it,
Whether it might be a vague shadow
That grows until it overwhelms all—
The day when all things, even emotions,
Are put up for sale, when everyone stops talking
Because everything has been said;

When man, no longer able to stay still,
Will be suspended in continuous movement—
His motion, like water in a glass, become theoretical
Because one place is the same as any other,
Or will it be the world-wide cataclysm
Everyone foresees will take place,
Prepared by his own hands; somehow
When it is so close, almost familiar part
Of the day, it no longer seems like doom.

It has been so long in coming, so often
Predicted without any dire results, some
Are beginning to feel it won't come at all;
Possibly that is when it happened—
When you stopped expecting it;
It may be just that: you will feel nothing—
You will put on a tie and walk out into it
As you would on any other day.

THEODORE HOLMES

LETTER FROM NEW HAMPSHIRE

now
it would be then
that walking down a snowy road
in the afternoon
under a gray sky
in winter
after it had snowed and would snow
but not yet

when the fir trees by the roadside
with week-old snow clumps
lying iced and heavy down
along the branches
and the twigs of bright green needles
clipped by passing plows
detached and crazy
littering
the too smoothed icy ground

it would be then
just coming into view of
a cottage bouncing up and down
but soon set straight
against the powdered mountain
banked up
on a dense horizon

it would be then
my dear
when thinking started up
to tell me how I missed you
now

that suddenly
the sky ran thin
with speckled afterlight
almost promising
it would not snow today
tonight

it would be then
at first starting of my thinking
of you
that there should negligently
fall into my head
the thought of this grave
heavy handsome
useless world

not needing me
for needing you
for needing me
in boots that leave
their stippled prints in snow
and eyes that take
this crystal quiet in
so quick and slow
and all this
with me or without
should not mean a thing
not anything at all

and when I thought this
then
the sky took back its worried look
grew solid gray
no different than before
except that now
that then

the first few flakes
stirred light
along my sleeve
like afterthoughts of easy living
easy dying
that would later be a heavy fall

it was then my dear
I missed you most
it was then that now
seemed lost the most

it was forever
then

EDWIN HONIG

BANG THE BARN AND THE HORSE RUNS OUT

Bang the barn and the horse runs out.
Sprawled. The madness of out. The tempest mane.
At the fence, she brakes, gathers herself and stands peeled.
Then she remembers the music of appeasement and her
    golden surge rings the yard
flying her colors.
Palomino.

Bang the barn and *she* runs out of the house.
Yaw. Yaw. Yaw. A tree of arms.
The splotch yell. "Get out of here!"
But then she turns and, leaning over the fence,
    all limp with tenderness,
with summer sounds
woos.

And the horse wheels and curves direct into her arms,
lolling its mane. She holds between the slabs
    of her palms
the long satin face with its neat fit. Even a boy
is sobered to see the old butt graced, abundant in the
    want of her hands
the mushroom loveliness
of the palomino.

DOROTHY HUGHES

THE POET AGEING

The new generation informs me
that our licence expires in time,
but appear uneasy and do not answer
when I ask them to name the year.

I'd have to admit the machine falters
hemming its neat and measured lines;
that something in the works that might
be a heart or a dynamo, jolts

and buckles on ordinary disasters,
like the morning one's woman walks off
to the beergarden and quietly swallows
the full bottle of memory-choking barbiturates.

One laughs more quietly, or screams to oneself
with the lips only slightly parted: the wail
on the street of the distancing ambulance
transports the body of love to the casualty ward:

saline drips in the vein a tide of silence.
Any knock on the door is a summons you'd rather
not answer. You know you will have to look
on what is not pretty, and what should not

be told will force you to want to talk.
At any time I'd be willing to hand in my cards
and call it a day, if only you could assure me
more age will spare me the feelings, terrors and tremors.

LOUIS JOHNSON

NARCISSUS, PHOTOGRAPHER

Mirror-mad,
he photographed reflections:
sunstorms in puddles,
cities in canals,

double portraits framed
in sunglasses,
the fat phantoms who dance
on the flanks of cars.

Nothing caught his eye
unless it bent
or glistered
over something else.

He trapped clouds in bottles
the way kids
trap grasshoppers.
Then one misty day

he was stopped
by the windshield.
Behind him,
an avenue of trees,

before him,
the mirror of that scene.
He seemed to enter
what, in fact, he left.

ERICA JONG

OCCASIONAL BIRDS

Morning, white as a sheet of paper,
I watch you with trepidation, still propped on my pillow,
Begin with a mist emitting occasional birds
Which seem to suggest (outside the world looks blind)
By moving so precisely there's some place
To go to when they leave the mist behind.

Pulling on socks I wonder
What are the chances today of being included
Just for one moment inside that syllabled silence,
Of feeling time, like a mammoth, steaming and black,
Lurch through the swamp not knowing there's a howdah
Of confident birds like jewels on its back.

Time moving, the bright birds still.
But morning fills the mind with too much noise.
Moth-memories come banging to get in.
I cram a casque over an empty skull
And face the mist—a morning like a wall.
An absent man gone walking in a pearl.

Verisimilitude: I take a child
Walking toward the slow-appearing trees.
His chatter sounds appropriate and wise,
Granting small features to a world born flat.
We walk inside the birthday of the world.
I wear his newness like a birthday hat,

Discern small things with him, begin
With smallness, stillness, as the skin of pearl
Thins round us and the sun pricks in.
Our tree becomes a wood. I see him ride,
Quite still, the back of time, I see him go.
I love his absence sitting by my side.

I love the trees revealed, the way
Light rinses fog from colors, opens out.
I love a size that does not care for me.
I have a skull so emptied that I float.
I love the vertigo! I love the cold!
Cold, I bend to button up his coat.

P. J. KAVANAGH

HEART'S LIMBO

I thrust my heart, in danger of decay
through lack of use,
into the freezer-compartment, deep
among the ice-cubes, rolls ready to brown 'n' serve,
the concentrated juice.

I had to remember not to diet on it.
It wasn't raspberry yoghurt.
I had to remember not to feed it to the cat
when I ran out of tuna.
I had to remember not to thaw and fry it.
The liver it resembled
lay on another shelf.

It rested there in its crystal sheath, not breathing,
preserved for posterity.

Suddenly I needed my heart in a hurry.
I offered it to you, cold and dripping,
incompletely thawed.
You didn't even wash its blood from your fingertips.
As it numbed them, you asked me to kiss your hands.
You were not even visibly frightened
when it began to throb with love.

Maimed, vicious as a ferret mutilated
by an iron trap set for bigger game,
dangerous, smooth as a young stone-bathing serpent,
nude, vulnerable as a new-hatched bird,
now my heart rests in your warm fingers' cage.

You anneal its pain with each caress.
You coax it with gentle sounds, in my strange language
nobody else has ever bothered to learn.
You nourish it with choice tidbits
from your enormous storehouse of love.

You smile when it beats in the rhythm of new music
we compose together, in the night.

You know my heart can never be re-frozen.
It would be leached of its flavor, taste like dust.
You know my heart can never be re-frozen.
It would rot as it thawed.
I would have it carted to the city dump
in its sealed refrigerator tomb.
But it will drum right to the end of you and me.
I have given you its lifetime guarantee.

CAROLYN KIZER

PHOTOGRAPHS OF OGUNQUIT

*Abbot Lot came to Abbot Joseph and said: Father,
according as I am able, I keep my little rule, and
my little fast, my prayer, meditation and contem-
plative silence; and according as I am able I strive
to cleanse my heart of thoughts: now what more
should I do? The elder rose up in reply and
stretched out his hands to heaven, and his fingers
became like ten lamps of fire. He said: why not be
totally changed into fire?*

*(The Wisdom of the Desert,
translated by Thomas Merton)*

1

On the last day you would not
let me take your picture. The sun
was shattering on glass,
the stonewharf hurt my eyes. I was angry
and the sky would not cloud over.

You were only twenty. It was the beginning
of the last day. The fishermen
refused to see the air between us,
the full face of your smile, the full
mouth, spitting. They sat eyeing the sea.

The wind ignited your hair. I resisted
your flight and walked away
way down the beach. The beach was full
of families. Your eyes were bluegreen.
Your distress was wild and anonymous.

I resisted your flight, now what more
must I do? The rocks hurt my eyes.
I was angry. I turned. The beach
was full of families. The fishermen
looked at their lines. Children are singing.

2

The curtains stood up and watched us,
the swollen door was forced shut, we were
warped against each other. I could not
tell you from the humid air. I wanted
to say I will not want to take your
picture to tell the truth I wanted to say
the sheets are smothering I
wanted to refuse to sleep against
the door I wanted to say the room
is standing in the corners holding its breath.
When it was over, neither of us laughed.

3

It was one o'clock. I'm not sure
how far I walked. You walked the wharf.
We walked back.

What you've given you cannot take
out of my hands, and what I've
given is still mine to give.
I take it with me, there is sand
in the shutter. Perhaps you meant
to leave it on the chair.

      We will fight back
with anger and recriminations,
with demands and ultimatums.
The camera is set on #4. The fishermen
saw nothing.
    I hope the bus has brought you
safely to yourself.
      When you wouldn't pose
you said "Now what more must I do?"
Children were singing.
      The camera
  is at the bottom of the suitcase.

PETER KLAPPERT

THE FISH

1

Beautiful
he landed
my hand upon him
blinded him
touched him as sail
touches wind
from under which he went
like ice
deep in his water
back to the river

where with luck
again
I hooked him
through appetite

through splashes
to the shore
clearing the air
as if it were not
medium enough

he came to rest
beneath the trees
the strangest thing

2

I thought of his courage
thought of his thought
freezing
through winter
to thaw in the heat
of his life and death
at the end of my sport
hook in his face

like the last piece
of puzzle
thawing his thought

moving him almost to tears
at this dying
cold scales
tail like a last card
flapping across the rocks
he had never seen
before
or my face above him
like a sun
to dry out his life

3

I had need then
to sit down together
me to my pause
he in a strange pasture
his cold body found
at last
on the rock cold as he is
my body pulling the cold
into my head

4

I knew him by what
he died by
not as one of the circle
deep in the water
not by a gesture
natural to himself
but rather how he had slipped
from the pool
to the world of different
breathers

5
Although I touched him
once
in my one life
felt his one life
tingle
looked at his magic guts
and felt them
cold

his gasping death
still grabs through rock
to mine

GREG KUZMA

AT EIGHTEEN

The grass is his; he is lord of greenness,
Especially of meadows lush and overgrown.
He is a prince of stones.
See how they skim the water, how they skip
Obedient to his wish,
And practised hand.
Larky as birds, he whistles up red leaves
In radiant galaxies.
The grain stands courtly in the sheaves
For his imperious love.
The stream receives his body as a god's.

Should he not laze, then, in mild weather
Among sweet-scented clover,
Spieling the names of daisies to the sun?
Be indolent as a cloud's shadow
Sailing the ruffled lake,
Or the enameled snake, asleep?
He is earth's fair-haired one
For whom the summer's minted and burned gold.
Venus, his gawky girl, lies down with him.

Lucky in love, as in animal grace,
Sleek as diving otters,
He fishes in green waters, or swims
The billows of the Queen Anne's lace.
There is no end to his possible kingdoms.
When hawks drive toward the sun's heart,
He is a wing unleashed,
And dreamy aerialist,
He could soar—

Why, then, is he heaped here,
Crumpled as junk iron, gone to rust,
In a bed neither green nor soft—
Earth's heir apparent
For whom grass tumbled and the sea swayed,
Sprawled in a bed made murderous and brutal
By blind machineries?
Here in the last kingdom,
His flashing provinces are overthrown,
The meadows taken,
And all those ring-bright pools
Where sun once struck medallions of his face.

JOAN LABOMBARD

CONFRONTATION WITH A STORK

More appropriate the stork should laugh at me
Than I make fun of his frayed evening suit,
Red-gaitered legs with shock-absorber joints,
The nodding of his almost voiceless head.

I share his air of shabbiness. He feels,
No doubt, rejected by his neighbor man,
Near whom he squatted, built his nest and fed,
Remained monogamous, domestic, friend,

Pretending to be midwife to the race,
Laboured for his keep devouring pests.
An egg-head chemist stuns with spray
The once green suburbs of his habitat.

The shaggy stance I recognise as in
A looking-glass. I settled near the gods,
Raised up cathedral spires to pierce the clouds
But heard no more than echo from the bells.

By strange mutation on this sewage farm
I watch the stork, deliberate and slow.
He stares at me, an exile from his trust,
Sensing the winter and the long flight home.

H. B. MALLALIEU

FIVE MINUTES TO NOON

Where did it come from,
water on all the streets?
At first thin as a membrane
in long sheets, it rose
with gentle insistence.
When scarce an inch deep,
it lapped up over each soft curb
like a film of crystal
to lick at the buildings' edges
with curious tongues.

Everyone's shoes
stopped and glittered
in the water
like cool emblems.
All distances
were short and long
in the same instant.

Suddenly everyone hailed
everyone else across
strangely elastic
corridors of water.
Long-haired boys with
flapping dungarees
and bare chests,
neither irony nor
instruction in their eyes,
hailed stolid businessmen.
Cops smiled hopefully
at drunkards,
and painfully beautiful women
smiled back warmly
at homebound lechers
whose eyes turned mild.

Without looking to the sky
or out to the city's rim,
you could tell that the sunlight
clung to the far edge
of each street's ribbon of water
while caressing its smooth expanse.
For a short time—time ceased.

MORDECAI MARCUS

NIGHT FRIENDS

Terror we expect, but we are always surprised by love.
—Thomas Williams.

What you taught me
and how I remember it
when I lie in the dark
I write on the cold trees.
I see what you see through the corners of my eyes.

Walking slowly,
we touch the empty silences
that lie in wait, settling to slow
decay.
We are here. These gray weathered branches
are facts.

You meet me, your eyes, your lips, your yellow
hair blown among long grasses.
There you are.
This is the way it seems to happen.

I am insane with words, with grief.
I am alone.
For two days now the one sound inside my head
has been your name.

S. J. MARKS

MYLAI CONVERSATION

Small Vietnamese boy, how old are you?
Six fingers, six years!
Why did you carry water to the wounded soldier?
Your father!
Your father, now dead, was enemy of free world.
You have given aid and comfort to enemy of free world.
You are now enemy of free world.
Who told you to carry water?
Your mother!
Your mother also is enemy of free world.
You go into ditch with your mother.
American politician has said
if we do not kill you as a boy, here,
in the elephant grass of Vietnam
we will have to kill you, as a man,
in the rye grass of U.S.A.
You understand, it is better to die
where you know the names of the birds
and trees and grass,
than in a strange country.
You will be number 128 in body count for today.
High body count will make commander-in-chief
of free world encouraged.
Good-bye, small six-year-old Vietnamese boy,
enemy of free world.

EUGENE J. McCARTHY

MASSACRE OF THE VILLAGERS

Grey-jawed, barricaded in the White House,
the President has been watching television,
an avid fan, tuned to the whack of players
deployed in random patterns on the grid;
he takes the stance of a gentleman pugilist.
"Socko, socko," he says. He is schooled
in calculating the appropriate response,
and suddenly there comes from his mouth:
"Gentlemen, let me say that . . ." He stops.
He has been watching himself too long.
His eyes click and roll like fruits
in the windows of a gambling machine.
In his mind there is an image he cannot help;
it is in a city or a village he thinks:
there are pigs' heads in windows, the faint
pink, pink, pink of mutton legs and tripe,
kidneys, hearts, sucklings smooth as babies,
and shoulders of something like cattle.
Beside him is his daughter who drifts about,
thin, cool, dreamy over nothing,
his image of how he'd have her be,
his remnant of passion.

JAY MEEK

THE GYM SHOES IN THE BACK OF MICHAEL'S CAR

That you are brown-haired, young, that permanence
continues to elude you in all things;
that Saturdays you sleep late, in the evening
take a date to a game, drive to a movie,

return much later, and alone, in darkness
seen, when seen, as at best an inconvenience,
not the not less than beautiful conveyance
into the single strangeness of your life

which somewhere it must be, should you permit it,
which will not happen here in just this fashion
for as long as these eyes sustain that vision
and for the miles of this intensive dreaming.

And that our shoes shall tell us, yours like little
arks on the local waters of indifference,
riding out tides of day and surfs of night
with total equanimity and patience,

waiting for life to claim them, for sheer presence
to flood and fill their spaces, quite possess them
as they have not before this been possessed,
asleep, consumed by dreams, and dreaming purpose.

That of the things that call to you in darkness
there is a breathing singularly yours,
a body which the evenings bring you into
and the bones stretch their limits to define;

later and deeper, where pure choice relents,
and who we could have been we have become,
the music and the meaning of that selfhood,
the substance of the gifts wrought for the other.

And that our shoes shall save us, could you know it,
you who are driving where the night falls deepest,
not knowing what to do with all that darkness,
not seeing mileage takes you to your life.

Tonight, across the street from where you sleep,
in a field drenched with fragrance, darkness, dreaming,
dusk is demanding some extreme transcendence
of most of us, receiving what it asks,

but for a little while no doubt will spare you
because of nights to come, and since your shoes,
vulnerable, exposed, adrift, and small,
make such a slender singing on the darkness.

HERBERT MORRIS

ZOO POEM

Certainly, my daughters, let us go to the zoo
and see all passions flattered in their cages.

Nothing too frightening, no Grand Guignol of emotions,
no bullring shambles, Roman Holiday, although
the smell in elephant and rhino houses
is disturbing. There will be moments when
I'll make you look aside.
                        The monkeys in particular
are unpredictable. But on the whole
this is acceptable, requires no turning off
as television news. Unlike our plays,
contains no comic traps, no countryman
who puns about the asp, or drunken porter
holding the doors against discoveries
of murdered guests.

    From here we're near enough
to tread the jungle's edge, yet pit and wire
protect us from the fangs, the monstrous rape.
The rancid breath presages no such death,
the sudden screaming, garments rolled in blood.

It's true the panther's nails
click on the concrete. Ticking pace by pace
he sends me to my watch, but simple hate,
I think, can't put the detonators back.
He's tricked, like all of us,
by time and place. What's broken lies
about him glittering, as magnesium licks
along a fusewire . . . For it's Here and Now
    to a bare bone,
so white it makes you blink your eyelids.

The sunlight and the bars
double the tiger's stripes. The plane tree's leaves
pattern the leopard twice. All this
is shadow play. We're daylight visitors,
unaltered by what shifts—leaves, sunlight, flies—
across the lines. Our glances never meet.
The roaming center of their gaze
     is elsewhere.
Only the incandescent heat
these creatures walk in may return
a gust of sudden burning
not to our temperate taste.

One troubled moment and we're set for going.
Linked up like elephants, we laugh, half reassured,
and join with strangers as they drift
down dusty lanes,
tranquil between the roars,
stale summer's ending,
to awaiting cars.

MICHAEL MOTT

THE INHABITANTS

This house is not ours
    and the land on which it sits
        belongs to the ants
who build pharaonic cities
    and regard mankind
        as only another
natural disaster,
    though our cat would argue,
        having established frontiers
which she patrols
    and tries to extend:
        on her own ground
she'll defy anything
    but if caught while infiltrating
        the neighbouring territory
will back off from a kitten,
    so strong is her belief
        in property rights
and national sovereignty,
    and the birds
        who probably think
of the earth
    as men think of the sea
        (it belongs to them but they
can never wholly
    belong to it),
        it's possible
to smile at the robins
    who look like
        Dickensian aldermen
as they play tug of war,
    a bird on one side,
        the whole planet on the other
and the worm
    caught in the middle,

but the nightjars
inhabit a darker
place in the mind,
for nothing kills
more quickly and cleanly:
it is as though
a piece of the sky
fell —
and lately an animal
has been raiding the garbage
and digging holes
in the garden,
a skunk, we think,
though we've never seen him;
going out after dark
I leave on the porchlight,
coming home
I keep to the path.

ALDEN NOWLAN

A FRIEND MOVING OUT OF OUR LIVES

back from the dark side of the earth
our friend has come to visit with us, for a few
                    days—
his face will not break, composed to earnest
conversation, the meeting of eyes that are not
                    pleading
for any kind of special love

he looks leaner than we remembered
there is something haggard in his young face
and he begins to speak of another year away
another year is all that is needed

but:
the innocence is weary, the ironies of old friends
stifled at half-smiles
he is carrying to that other continent
the sorrow of thirty years locked
in the same skeleton, behind the same
                    unhating American face
where so much hate has boiled, crazily—

why
why has no-one taught him to love properly?—
why has no one
scolded him into shape?—why is the carnal
                    kingdom of
husbands and wives a distant continent to him,
                    forbidding
entry?

the normal
smile constantly with their small American
                    smiles
knowing the rules
the absolute limits

he is baffled by his numerous loves
as by wasps darting
about his innocent head
he does not know that the rules of the game
                    declare:
two mates, two sexes, a tidy house and forms
to fill out for the government, proof of
                    normality
proof that the years pass in careful handfuls
in the perfect selfish kingdom of ordinary love

JOYCE CAROL OATES

THE CHILD WHO SKATES ALONE

Sometimes walking by winter ponds I
    find
Some child skating alone, his feet
Fashioning quick arcs on the dark
Mysterious arenas of ice,
And I know it is better if we do not
    meet.

For it is not so long ago—
Not long at all as the small ponds live
Or the thick pines crowding the shore,
Since I too buckled on my blades
And sailed across the forest floor.
And I have not forgotten yet
How fine it was to leap alone
Into the burning winter air
And feel the crystal leagues of space
Like inches fall defeated where
It seemed one had the sudden poise
And magic to go anywhere.

Once it happened that I turned
And found a stranger on the shore.
His smiling silence measured me —
I fell to where I was before.
Sometimes by country ponds I glimpse
A child who in his woolen warmth
Attacks the zenith like a swan —
In the fat pines that hug the shore
I choose some turning from that place,
And hurry on.

MARY OLIVER

WINTER RITE

Mother-of-pearl in cloud, the sun, low
Over the holy island; the straggle
Of sacred timber hunched and crook-back
For the dark months' long assailment;

And the lake where the god sprawls
Sleeping under rotted water-lilies
With weed clogged at his groin.
Safe fish weave basketries of bubbles

Through his fingers. Year in, year out,
In this sick season, we bring him
Offerings: spears, axes, sickle-blades,
Bronze scoops and bridle-bits.

We have given him prisoners for his drowned
Army, their screams at the knife
Sleep-songs for his still warriorship.
He is a god, he knows our service.

We have taken the great boar live
Then cast it into his pool, fenced it
With sacrificial arrows. It threshed
Until it died for his fresh food.

Year after year, before the god's lake
Freezes, we climb to his stone altars.
They tilt above the lilies that were gold
In summer. We face, despite our fears,

The god's invisible three faces.
We do not expect to see him. He allows
Us to approach and accepts our gifts
With the silence of all gods.

JOHN ORMOND

ON GIVING ADVICE TO TANYA

*who probably doesn't need it and if she did would be most unlikely
to take it*

Now that you're five years old and going to school,
learning the facts, being led gently amongst soups
and mixed vegetables—as one not yet able to walk
alone, whose feet are easily bruised—I watch your
progress (your conditioning, programming, your being taught
the whys and wherefores, the hows and how-nots)
and wish for the impossible, to tell you about yourself,
to act as senselessly as one who lifts mermaids
out of the Gulf's warm stream, who wants to store them
safely in some unobtainable deep-freeze.

                                        Thus, while
you're being told tales of kings, of kingly loyalties,
of principalities and powers, the mistranslated history
of our helpless race, I think of how—so often—
you seem older than your years, leap up and rush blindly
towards discovery, of how your best and brightest hopes
will be undone, expectancy become obscured in casual
summer fires, of your pain (which I share) . . . and privately
I hope you'll come to know that somewhere there are oceans
and ships and travelling and maybe nowhere to arrive—
and I visualise your travelling and wonder what kind of sense
you'll make of it, whether you'll make any kind of sense
of it at all.

And sometimes I imagine I can talk to you,
that an unknown genius has invented us a common syntax
and vocabulary, that we can actually converse, make
mutual and meaningful exchange, that I can present
as gifts to you, fragments of myself—a clockwork mouse,
a piece of string, the burnt-out offerings of whim and will.
But these are fantasies and dreams, the psyche's slow
meanderings by mountain, valley and threatening hill,
for water will wake you, its reflections suggest dancing
and drowning—the outward not the inner view—
and you'll believe there are years to be used, centuries
to waste, time enough for the most fastidious to debate
abstruse questions of tenure . . . of ownership
and being owned.

      Because no suitable vocabulary
has been invented yet, I work with the grammar of
Andersen and Grimm, stretch it out, ransack mythology,
adapt and plagiarise at will, try to remember
the day I saw, temporarily contained within
their private universe and free of human fear
and guilt, some children on a swing, recognise
I should have found some profundity for you in this—
yet there's nothing to be said. You know the obvious,
and the other thing you'd best discover for yourself.

A. I. H. PATERSON

SO GOOD OF THEIR KIND

"Snakes hanging from a tree!
Snakes hanging from the rough crack-willow bark!
Snakes hanging—come and see—
It almost frightened me—
I passed and saw them, shining in the dark."

Not snakes, huge slugs. They hung
Twined in sevenfold embrace, by a tough slime:
Strong slime that held them wrung
Together, swinging and strung
In the great double helix of our time,

And there suspended, till
They had accomplished what they had to do.
And though they seemed so still,
It was dynamic will
That held them, and their world about them too.

Fissured and frowning rock
Behind and overhanging, the bole seemed,
But strong desire had struck
That too; each ridge and nook
With something glittering and precious gleamed:

There must have been some dance,
Some festal wooing, for the rugged face
With nacreous phosphor glanced,
Festooned with radiance:
And so they had adorned their nuptial place.

A great electric tide
Flowed through my flesh, so honoured to have seen them;
All life was on their side,
Death was so well defied—
And then I saw a wonder grow between them.

Something—a great round gem—
Seemed from the two twined bodies to be growing;
Flower on a double stem,
The soul of both of them,
Each lost, both consummated in one knowing.

It flowered and faded; rest
Took them a moment, as they hung entwined
And vulnerable; at best
Their strength was of the least,
They had achieved their height; their star declined.

One wreathed himself away,
Climbing the wonderful rope. The other soon
Devouring the strong grey
Bond of their nuptial day
Followed; and with strange swiftness both were gone.

But one on the rough rind
Turning towards his fellow as they moved,
Eager to seek his blind
Safe crevice, yet could find
A moment for the mate whom he had loved:

With almost courtly pause,
Bending the head with almost conscious grace,
Seeming to know the laws
By which life pleads love's cause,
With the soft mouth-parts touched the other's face.

RUTH PITTER

GIRAFFE

The only head in the sky.
Buoyed like a bird's,
on bird legs, too.
Moves in the slowmotion
of a ride
across the long-legged miles
of the same place.
Grazes in trees.
Bends like a bow
over water
in a shy sort of
spreadeagle.
Embarrassed by
such vulnerability,
often trembles, gathering
together
in a single moment
the whole loose
fragment of body
before the run downwind.
Will stand still
in a camouflage of kind
in a rare daylight
for hours,
the leaves spilling
one break of sun
into another,
listening to the lions.
Will, when dark comes
and the fields open
until there are
no fields,

turn in the length
of light
toward some calm
still part of a tree's
new shadow, part of the moon.
Will stand all night
so tall
the sun will rise.

STANLEY PLUMLEY

THOMAS HARDY AT WESTBOURNE PARK VILLAS

Not that I know where in this changed district
He may have walked under unwarming sun
Through a hedged righteousness already bricked
Up to the pale sky and the many chimneys clouding it,
    Nor where black steeple, tar-gate and gun-
bright anthracite held back the Spring and the exact green
      to bring it.

Though the smoke's gone now, the old frailty shows
    In the blankness of people coming out of doors
Hardly renumbered since his time: each house knows
As many stories as in the iron sublime we call
    Victorian. Suicide, lost love, despair are laws
of a visiting Nature raging against proof and practice
      and changing all.

Here, rather than in death-filled Dorset, I see him,
    The conspirator against the gods
Come to the capital of light on his own grim
Journey into darkness: the dazzle would tell
    Him these were the worst of possible odds—
ordinary gestures of time working on faces the watermark
      of Hell.

PETER PORTER

THE SHADOWS

After forty the shadows start to fall.
I think of a few friends
On whom the encroaching darkness descends.

There was one who stared for hours at a wall,
Lying on an iron bed,
With a weight lurching about in his head.

Another, plunging into alcohol,
Found it as bitter as
The lees of sex, the soured wine of the Mass.

A third gulped down fistfuls of seconal
But was still not granted
The long sleep that he had always wanted.

A stomach pump dredged him: a hospital
Passed six shocks through his brain;
A good psychiatrist tried to explain

The root of his trouble was Oedipal.
Though he still cannot sleep
He has some inkling of what makes him weep.

Our own darkness shelters daimons who call
Till we take the long spiral
Down to a stifling, self-created hell.

I too have watched the shadows growing tall.
May light perpetual
Shine on the haunted and redeem us all.

JOHN PRESS

AFTER MELVILLE

for Bett and Walter Bezanson

1

The sea-coast looks at the sea, and the cities pour.
The sea pours embassies of music: murder-sonata, birth-sonata,
the seashore celebrates the deep ocean.

Ocean dreaming all day all night of mountains
lifts a forehead to the wakes of stars;
one star dives into a still circle: birth, known to all.

A shore of the sea, one man as the shore of the sea;
one young man lying out over configurations of water
never two wave-patterns the same, never two same dreamings.

He writes these actualities, these dreamings,
transformed into themselves, his acts, his islands,
his animals ourselves within his full man's hand.

Bitter contempt and bitter poverty,
Judaean desert of our life, being locked
in white in black, a lock of essences.

Not graves not ocean but ourselves tonight
swing in his knowledge, his living and its wake,
travelling in the sea that goes pouring, dreaming

where we flash in our lifetime wave, these breathing shallows
of a shore that looks at the deep land, this island
that looks forever at the sea; deep sexual sea
that breathes one man at the shoreline of emergence.
He is the sea we carry.

2

They come into our lives, Melville and Whitman who
ran contradictions of cities and the one-sparing sea
held in the long male arms—Identify.

They enter our evenings speaking—Melville and Crane
taking the wars of our parentage, silence and smoke,
tearing the live man open till we wake.

Emily Dickinson, Melville in our breathing,
isolate among powers, telling us the sea
and the slow dance of the absence of the sea.

Hawthorne whose forehead knew the revelation—
how can we receive the vision at noonday?
Move with the revelation? Move away?

More violent than Melville diving the sea deeper
no man has ever gone. He swims our world
violence and dream, safe only in full danger.

3

A woman looks at the sea.
 Woman in whose waiting is held ocean
 faces the other sea where his life drowns and is saved,
 recurrent singing, the reborn wave.

A man looking into the sea.
 He sails, he swims among the opposites,
 diving, making a life among many unknowns,
 he takes for his knowledge the future wake of stars.

The sea looking and not looking.
 Among the old enemies, a transparent lake.
 Wars of the sea and land, wars of air;   space;
 against the corroded wars and sources of wars, a lake of being
                                                          born.

A man and a woman look into each other.
 One man giving us forever the grapes of the sea.
 Gives us marriage; gives us suicide and birth; he drowns
 for the sake of our look into each other's body and life.
 Allowing the great life: sex, time, the feeding powers.
 He is part of our look into each other's face.

MURIEL RUKEYSER

A YOUNG AMERICAN IN ROME

Bernini, Salvi, frivolous, lavish,
their fountains flow over the plains
of Kansas, wiping out the sober corn
(*long for the sunrise and the cloudless sky*)
silver silos obliterate the watery plumes.

    Not for the Greek or Slav the Forum stands
    the shrine of order but Franklin
    and Voltaire laid out the streets of downtown
    America by rigid Roman rule
    and dust blows up hot on Pine and Elm, dries out the heart.

He turns from the rows of corn pushing
through the marble slabs. From the top
of the column of the Immaculate
Conception views the basilica, the
sweep of the piazza (*up there is the
Pope's apartment*). The whole thing is a heartless arid

    Unending night, the same water pumped through
    for ever—a fool's wit. Give me
    happiness. Sì, padre: tomorrow in
    Ravenna (*in the blue gold mist of
    Galla Placidia*) I break with Mitzi.
    Three months, Father: no love, no heart. Give me happiness.

Figlio mio: we dont sell happiness.
That is something you have to find
yourself without looking for it. Your sins
are the least of your troubles. It is not
time yet for you to think of them. First you
must find your heart. Learn to give. Learn to be hurt. Grow. Weep.

Over the mountains and to Ravenna
(*to Galla Placidia and gold*
stars in the blue night and ghost ships sailing
on the Adriatic) to break with Mitzi.
What is the shape of a heart that is emptied of love

that was never there? Perhaps a tessera
lodged in it stops the flow of blood
of frivolous water pumps through for ever.
But it must break and the blood flow out mixed
with water; nourish the tall corn: fill the silver silos.

EDWARD SARMIENTO

DESTINATIONS

The train stood on the line
Stock still, like a long factory.
It hummed inside with impatience,
Indignation and anxiety.
"A mechanical fault," the Guard said,
Omniscient and complacent.

Fretfulness prickled and simmered.
A passenger read a letter
Again and again and he groaned
With an anguish no words could utter.
She had written: "If you do not come
I will never see you again."

Another cursed British Railways,
Complained he would miss his plane
That left at noon for Canberra.
And he did. The delinquent train
Was fifty minutes late on arrival,
Foiling both flyer and lover.

But the plane to Canberra crashed,
Its entire mortal cargo burnt
And scattered like fertilizer
Over acres of land and paper
To feed the living with feelings
Of relief, grief and terror.

The lover lost his girl,
She was taken by a sly watcher:
So because that train was late
A heart broke like a pitcher
But a life was saved from the fire
To balance the scales of fate.

A year later the case is changed:
The reprieved passenger dead
Of a slow and mauling pain;
The lover in a happy bed—
The girl he longed for turned shrew—
Blesses the unpunctual train.

VERNON SCANNELL

TOWARD THE END OF WINTER

for Galway Kinnell

I lie a frozen field waking
hunchbacked, my skin the shell of an egg.

Light opens its wings over my infant body.
I flake, seeing my hands again
for the first time.

I go out making fresh tracks,
touch each stone twice, bury
my sleep-rotted skin under new grass.

And whistle, biding my time toward spring.
Leaves, leaves break from my breath.

PHILIP SCHULTZ

THE ARTISAN AS HERO

1. THE ARROW-MAKER

Forget art, never mind
the brain or the brawn.
It doesn't go back
to the wisest or best,
understand—the one who scratched
pictures on the cave wall or made
wild guesses on the lay of the bones,
nor even the biggest
and strongest. It goes back
to the clever-fingered brute
who sharpened the first stone.

It starts there and it's that simple.
There had to be something
that mattered more than anything else,
and the one thing that mattered
that much to any man
was one more day at any price.
Take it from there and you see
why they let him sit in the shade—
him of the funny knack—
fooling with sticks and stones.
Back of the stupid eyes,
deep in the earliest brow,
they knew what the thinkers
still can't think around.

2. THE POTTER

Jug, bowl, cup, bottle—
no cunning gets you past
the basic cave and entrance.
So let's say it was a she,
though we can't guess
how many thousands of years
she bent over the curved leaf,

the cupped hand,
the cleft in the wood
that kept the water—
and nothing went pop
in the slow thick porridge
at the top of her skull.

And perhaps never did.
Though at last she picked up
the handful of mud
and happened to shape it
round and holding. Later
saw it lying where she'd dropped
it—sun-baked and full of water.
So did it again and went
picking berries with it,
and never knew she had bumbled
onto civilization.

It's still in a mothering
of hands, a craft of caress,
as the wheel turns,
that the shape takes place.

3. THE WEAVER

It came late. It's sophisticated,
a luxury. Skins, crude knots and lashings
were adequate. They didn't
really need this. And somebody
had to think two things at once
before it could happen.
Somebody had to notice the mystery
of opposites: dark and light,
male and female, earth and sky.
Somebody had to feel the split
of good and evil in his gut.
Somebody had to sadden
on separation.

It moves away from mere
usefulness. It gets
abstract. Don't let fish nets,
traps and baskets confuse
what the troubled one was up to
when he sat plaiting
two thongs or reeds, making
nothing in particular that time,
but easing an ache
he barely knew he had.

Among pots and arrows,
somebody had begun
the long agony
of reconciliation.

R. E. Sebenthall

PROLOGUE

First, as you enter the room, you will be aware
Of one thing only: the colour of the walls, the floor, the ceiling.
It will be white, unglaring, and of an eggshell finish.
You will find it unnerving though not unduly ominous.
To begin with it will seem not so very dissimilar
From rooms you have entered before. These, however,
Will rarely, if at all, have been white under your feet.
The texture of these white surfaces will be uniform.
As you adjust to this you will also become aware
That the door by which you entered has totally merged
With the white wall. And that there are no windows.

The next noticeable thing will concern your own person,
Or rather the clothes in which you are dressed. They have become
White like the room and completely encase you
In a suit of what might be white polystyrene.
Of course you are unable to see your face or the back of your head
And that causes you some disquiet. Especially you wonder
About the colour of your eyes. You begin to blink rapidly.
These small moments of non-whiteness do not comfort you.
Apart from yourself the room will at first seem empty,
But that is illusion. You will discover, more by sense than sight,
That it contains an object: A small white cube.

Curiously enough you will at first refrain from touching it
Though unaware of the reason. You will kneel down
And gaze upon it for a long time. Because there are no shadows
You will not at once discover that it possesses a small groove
Encircling it some one and a half inches from the top.
Not till you touch it with your fingers will you know this.
So, it may be a box, a box with no fastener.
However the lid, if it is a lid, refuses to lift,
Though refusal, for such an inanimate block, is a word
Too human and personal; say, rather, it will not move.
Therefore it may be merely a solid cube of wood.

Again you are at fault, for you have no possible means
Of telling from its whiteness the substance of which it is made;
Its weight is no guide. Nor, when you shake it, does it rattle.
You will spend a long time manipulating this cube
Though you will not know whether it is a second or a year.
You will be unaware of the usual functions of the body.
It may be that you will carry it to various places
Within the silence of your room. Silence?
Ah, that is another thing; you will begin to confuse
The whiteness with silence. When that happens
You will not know whether you have seen colour or heard a sound.

Immediately you will begin to wonder
Whether anything happened or not. You will wait
Concentrating your entire being on the situation.
Was there noise? Was there colour? You will return.
You will replace the cube in the exact position
From which you removed it. You will back to a wall.
If a door has opened you will not know. Except:
There has been a change. Has there been a change?
It is a pity there is no one you can discuss it with
Though it is doubtful whether any conversation
Would move you a degree nearer to understanding.

First, you will be aware, entering the other room,
If indeed you have entered, of one thing only:
The colour of the walls, the floor, the ceiling
Will be textureless black. You will examine your body
Though you will be unable to see your face or the back of your head.
In the exact centre of the room you will discover. Yes.
Oh, and by the way, please don't worry yourself about the names
We use when trying to baptise God. Eventually you will move
To a wall where a door may open or may not open.
You may listen, if you wish, hoping that God might speak.
But that, of course, is a very different matter.

JOHN SMITH

OLD APPLE TREES

Like battered old mill hands, they stand in the orchard—
Like drunk legionnaires, heaving themselves up,
Lurching to attention. Not one of them wobbles
The same way as another. Uniforms won't fit them—
All those cramps, humps, bulges. Here, a limb's gone;
There, rain and corruption have eaten the whole core.
They've all grown too tall, too thick, or too something.
Like men bent too long over desks, engines, benches,
Or bent under mail sacks, under loss.
They've seen too much history and bad weather, grown
Around rocks, into high winds, diseases, grown
Too long to be willful, too long to be changed.

Oh, I could replant, bulldoze the lot,
Get nursery stock, all the latest ornamentals,
Make the whole place look like a suburb,
Each limb sleek as a teenybopper's—pink
To the very crotch—each trunk smoothed, ideal
As the fantasy life of an adman.
We might just own the Arboreal Muscle Beach,
Each tree disguised as its neighbor. Or each disguised
As if not its neighbor—each doing its own thing
Like executives' children.

                              Oh, at least I could prune.
At least I should trim the dead wood; fill holes
Where the rain collects and decay starts. Well, I should;
I should. There's a red squirrel nests here someplace.
I live in the hope of hearing one saw-whet owl.
Then, too, they're right about spring. Bees hum
Through these branches like lascivious intentions. The white
Petals drift down, sift across the ground; this air's so rich
No man should come here except on a working pass;
No man should leave here without going to confession.

All fall, apples nearly crack the boughs;
They hang here red as candles in the
White oncoming snow.

Tonight we'll drive down to the bad part of town
To the New Hungarian Bar or the Klub Polski,
To the Old Hellas where we'll eat the new spring lamb;
Drink good mavrodaphne, say, at the Laikon Bar,
Send drinks to the dancers, those meatcutters and laborers
Who move in their native dances, the archaic forms.
Maybe we'll still find our old crone selling chestnuts,
Whose toothless gums can spit out fifteen languages,
Who turns, there, late at night, in the center of the floor,
Her ancient dry hips wheeling their slow, slow tsamikos;
We'll stomp under the tables, whistle, we'll all hiss
Till even the belly dancer leaves, disgraced.

We'll drive back, lushed and vacant, in the first dawn;
Out of the light gray mists may rise our flowering
Orchard, the rough trunks holding their formations
Like elders of Colonus, the old men of Thebes
Tossing their white hair, almost whispering,

> Soon, each one of us will be taken
> By dark powers under this ground
> That drove us here, that warped us.
> Not one of us got it his own way.
> Nothing like any one of us
> Will be seen again, forever.
> Each of us held some noble shape in mind.
> It seemed better that we kept alive.

W. D. SNODGRASS

THE RISING

The mushrooms are rising, leaving home
with dignity, and won't say why—
the great crocodilus, the shaggymanes,
passing like minor orders of angels
at change of shift—the weeping lactaria:
boletes with tilted hats: beautiful
vile amanitas, scarlet women:
tumbling puffballs, little moons.
And the common agaricus upward snows;
the yellow shelvers, brilliant sails,
are easing out of the skins of branches;
the lesser clavaria slowly mounting
like needles drawn to a higher force,
a fuller magnet, a crystalline sphere
where nothing exists but the thought of peace.
And the moss already stirs, the grass—
how long before an oak will loosen
aloft, borne on a lift of leaves
in a rain of clods?—but no, the clods
will be rising, entire savannahs, level
communes of flowers, ferns; cows
will darken the sky above Ohio.
For now, the mushrooms, the true with the false
morels, the chanterelles, tiny trumpets
causing no sound: no sound: no sound:
going away.

BARRY SPACKS

RAIN

This morning, waking to the firm
dictum of water,
the house submitting like an invalid,
the mattress turning over and going back to sleep,

the oven brooding its load of bread,
things growing quietly in the cellar,
my hands clenched like roots,
I refuse the warm huddle and go out.

Locking eyes with the mist
the garden challenges,
sticks and stones pricking
up through the rain, steady, brown,

and macadam is shining. Excited,
the streets breathe rapidly.
Bird feathers, leaves
are cleared: the greedy drinking of gutters,

a thirst nailing the ground
into dark patterns.
Crosses, swastikas, no matter;
I am drawn to them, lulled, unjudging,

undergoing villages without a sign,
vast highways swishing
by, the hiss of wet car wheels,
the water wandering, the continental

divide. Strangers,
there is no name on my body;
the rain soothes like unanswerable
questions, the roads, toward some revelation,

overflow; the wanderer, urgent,
hurries through rivers.
Blood rises in waves in response to the wet;
the rich steam moist in the air,

the fields, loam and manure mixing,
exhaling under their blanket,
the chickens flurrying and niggling,
the grey boxes of band-aids, the cities:

the whole earth sliding in the downward
direction. Where do you run, roads,
lush with water? To what meeting
of cabalistic signs?—To the torrent;

to the unburdening. To the confessional
down by the ocean. The water foams there
like a leap of the heart: I spring
with the lake fish for land-locked release.

KATHLEEN SPIVACK

SUMMER IN FAIRBANKS

is like a dull dream. From time to time
the paper boy comes grinning with proof that
something has happened after all. Here
where the highways end. To go north
from here, you must be a bird or wealthy.
The prospectors have each been starved and strained
away down southward and to old folks homes.
Here is where the nights end too. Never
to sense the dark for days is strange, and not
so hot as one might think. It is strange
always to be able to see, and say:
that is there and that is there and that
is over there, always. Strange, not to tell
the end of days by any other way
than clocks, and meals; televisions turning off.
Different, for things to seem
to the eye like one day, that somehow
has slowed down to months, years, icebergs
of minutes so separated by an absence
from anything that ever came before,
that the anxious people find themselves
waiting for the swish on their lime lawns
of the dirty tennis shoes of
the grinning paper boy who brings them yesterday.

LEON STOKESBURY

TO LAURA PHELAN: 1880-1906

Drunk I have been. And drunk I was that night
I lugged your stone across the other graves,
to set you up a hundred yards away.
Flowers I found, then. Drunk I have been.
And am, standing here with no moon to spill
on the letters of your name; my loud fingers
feeling them out. The stone is mossed over.
And why must I bring myself in the dark
to stand here among the sour grasses
that stain my white jeans? Drunk I have been.
See, the thick dew slides on the trees, wet weeds,
wetness smears the air; and a vague surf
of wildflowers pushes my feet, slipping
close to my legs. When the thought comes at last
that people fall apart, that the things we do
will not do. Ends. Then, we come to scenes
like this. This scene of you. You apart:
this is not you; and yet, this is where I stand
and close my eyes, and feel the ragged wind
blow red and maul my hair. In the night somewhere,
dandelions foam. This is not you. Drunk
I have been. Across this graveyard, that
is where you are. Yet I stand here. Would ask
things of your name. Would wish. Would not be told
of the stink in the skull, the eye's collapse.
Would be told something new, something unknown.—
A mosquito bites my hand. The only sound
is the rough wind. Drunk I have been,
here, at the loam's maw, before this stone
of yours, which is not you. Which is.

LEON STOKESBURY

TO JANIS JOPLIN

In the days of drugs
In the drowsy season, sunless, season of sleep
She flung herself deadened
Down among the trash
Behind the rush of buildings and business
Back into the hidden
Deep into corners, comfortless
And black

Fate had cast her grief into sound
And she learned to sing like the lost
A language garbled with garbage,
Learned to hear like the lonely
The silent screams of light, piercing
And pulsing in the neon night
Her night
Longing and black

She was a white child, a child of deep white tears
Whose clear white sweat melted her flesh
Into the flashing lights that held her
A child of white affluence and a pale unimpassioned God
Who tried to redeem feelings she was not ashamed to claim
A child running from riches
And unloading affluent feelings into blues, devil songs
Black songs

She sang, a fine rude delicate uncouth miracle
Her cries were improvised on our sorrow
She drew us near, and we who had left our dead
From Jackson to Kent
Listened
As she sang us her devil songs
Sang us ourselves
Sang us black.

CAROLYN J. SUMNER

FOR BUFFY SAINTE-MARIE

Suddenly
       she
          looks
       a thousand years old
    with just that violence
        kick of the wind
            her leg gives sideways
     her grin breaking from tanned
        drum of her face
   taut nose
body half-bent
        lance   jack-knife
howl in the voice
    as if the stars had grown violent
        suddenly   on an impulse

   then
quick as hawk from throne
           or wren from hiding
              or still small wind of summer
     in the nostrils of the dead
            her confidence
      friendship in ghostly eyes
         blue of cut turquoise

  no
    well of sweet water
        no
         fish blood
     from a very old
         very old
           sea

black bear comes out of a sigh
        cloud as small as a paw
     on the horizon
              it is the distance
      not the white   not the law
             not the treaty
  not the ghosts who walk out of battle
        with noses to the ground
  but the walls
      more dangerous than stone
     thin as paper
      meeting back to back
      the trackless wastes
    so distanced from each other that they meet
              now back to back

  bears
      mountain-lions
          death   in their paws
     in their embrace
           bigger than we have been

it is November in the month of the dead
    and the dust begins to rise a little from the roads
      omen of distant summer
  it is as if the dead   blew on the roads
         when the rains are over
    as they walk by   looking down hill
         and the dust responds a little

she stomps in this country
      and everyone goes native now
         out to the streets
  with the smell of our fear on the wind
perhaps   we will all get killed soon

                NATHANIEL TARN

CHILDREN AT EVENING

It's growing dark. The children play
At hide-and-seek as if the day would last
Forever; forever is a long, long time to hide
Under the bush and never breathe while at your side
A breathless thing is waiting for the vast
Curtain of dusk; then it will say

I'm It, and I've been watching you
And you can never hide from me, or hold
Your breath. I am the breath you breathe, the bush whose mien
Takes on the graduations of a darker green
Subtly as the hunted sun grows cold,
Hiding no matter what you do

To find it. Children hope, but night
Will put them all to bed, now that things
Slowly diminish and the outlines shift and change
And even walls of houses shudder and grow strange;
This is the evening, and the evening brings
An end to childish appetites

When faces merge into the leaves
They hide behind, and wait to hear the call
Quavering up, "Allee allee outs-in-free"
From where the seeker stands beside the silent tree.
Then they'll come in because they are so small,
To sleep and drain the sea with sieves.

JOHN TAYLOR

ON INSECTS

As they pass in the labyrinthine buried walks
Of their interminable nests beneath the mounds
Of farfetched twigs, the earnest ants
Stop jerkily, confront each other, and then touch.
Touch, touch, they say, here is myself
And that is you, or, put it in another way,
Here's you, and that encased in your black carapace
Is me. Touch. Touch.
                    The bees
Fill up their time with similar small talk.
It is epiphany to dance the route
To Sunday morning's aster levulose,
But this is seldom. Most of what the hive
Contains is vibratory small talk. Touch.
It is in contact that we maintain
And pass along our life.
Touch.
Live again.

LEWIS THOMAS

CHILD'S DRAWING OF A HOUSE

Come, let us live there
it is a blue house
and the yellow rays of the yellow sun
reach right down to the roof.
The door of the house
is just about to open
and the window is crooked with happiness.
There is a purple bird flying by
and 3 purple daisies and 1 red daisy
growing by the door step.

Why do you hesitate
surely life there would be rich as custard.
It would be possible to play a violin there.
And I'm sure there is a garden
out behind the house
strawberries, cool leafy lettuce
onions like little moons.
And at night the silver rays
of the silver moon
would reach right down to the roof.

No, you say, we are not allowed
to live there
never in this world allowed.
See, there isn't even a gate
to that place.

EVELYN THORNE

THE WEED GARDEN

I am the ghost of the weed garden.
 Stalk among stones—you will find me
remembering husks and pods, how crisp burdock
 couches in the moon for every passer.
  I am the dry seed of your mind.

 The hour will strike when you dream me, your
  hand at the sheet like five thin hooks.
I will wait for you in the old vines rattling on
 the wind, in the ground-pine. I will show you
  where rue has blossomed and eyebright,

 mother-thyme. You must name me Yarrow.
  Bitter vetch shall catch your step as
you follow, hearing the stars turning to crystal,
 sweet lovage turning sere, adder's tongue and
  Jew's-ear at their whisper. Nightshade

 will consume the beautiful lady.
  Dwarf elder, dodder-of-thyme, I
am the thing you fear in the simple of your blood:
 toothwort in the dust, feverfew, mouse-ear,
  sundew and cup-moss, tormentils.

LEWIS TURCO

FOR A MAN WHO DIED IN HIS SLEEP

Once in, he can stay as long as he remembers
To lock the door behind him, being afraid
Of nothing within the ordinary passage
Where he hangs his hat and coat, thinking of bed.

Hs feels as safe as houses: the predictable ceiling,
The floor at its level best, the walls, the windows
Beyond which the sky, under glass, is slowly streaming
Harmlessly westward with its tricks and shadows,

And, going upstairs, he lies down to be soft
In a nest of boxes fitted against the night.
He shuts his lids like theirs and, wrapped like a gift,
Presents himself to sleep, to be opened by daylight.

At first, there is nothing, then something, then everything
Under the doors and over the windowsills
And down the chimney, through the foundation, crawling
From jamb to joist and muttering in the walls,

And he lies tongue-tied under the gaping roof
Through which the weather pours the news of his death;
In sheets and lightning, the broken end of his life
Comes pouring crown fire through the roof of his mouth,

And now he dreams he is dreaming that he knows
His heart's in the right place, safe, beating for good
Against the beams and braces of his house
All the good nights to follow, knocking on wood.

DAVID WAGONER

THE OTHER SIDE OF THE MOUNTAIN

To walk downhill you must lean partially backwards,
Heels digging in,
While your body gets more help than it can use
In following directions—
Because it's possible simply to fall down
The way you're going
Instead of climbing against it. The baffling dead ends
Of traveling upward
Are turned around now, their openings leading down
To the land you promised
Yourself, beyond box canyons and blind-draws.
They branch repeatedly,
But the direction you choose should be as easy to take
As your right hand.
The sky is a constant; even its variables
Like cirrus and cumulus
Will cancel each other out in a rough balance,
Taking turns at weather.
The wind may bluff and bluster and cut corners
Or skip a whole valley,
But eventually it has nothing to do with you,
Not even when it throws
The dust of your own country in your eyes.
At dawn, at darkness,
The sun will be here or there, fullface, rearview;
It evens out in the end.
You must keep your goal in mind as clear as day
Though it doesn't matter
What you may think it looks like: second sight
Is simply perseverance;
And getting there from here is a set of stages
Demanding candlepower,
Foot-pounds and simple levers, thirst and hunger.
Signposts are seasonal
And not forensic: one end may come to a point

And the other be indented,
But the words will be gone, and the rusty earth and air
Will have eaten the pole and nails.
You must take time to notice what grows on rocks
Or squeezes between them—
The gnawing lichen, bone-weed and thorny scrub—
All hanging tough
And gnarling for elbow room or squatters' rights.
These are the straighteners,
The levelers at work on the thick and crooked:
Some distant species
Will find the world made flat by the likes of these.
You must do your bit
By scuffing downhill heel-first on behalf of erosion,
For the sake of another time
When the mountains are made plain and anyone standing
Can see from here to there
Without half trying. When your shoes are out of step
And your clothes are a burden
And you feel bone-tired, sit down and look around.
You're there. No matter what
You had in mind as a proper circumstance,
You've come to it at last:
A rock-strewn slope from which you have a view
Of a farther rock-strewn slope.
You can pick up dust in your hand and let it fall.
The place is real.
You can bite a grass-stem, look, take a deep breath
And, naturally, let it go.

DAVID WAGONER

HAPPINESS

Suddenly, I thought of Christmas.
Not the Christmas of the demonstrative shooting-star
nor the cold, still, and achingly beautiful Christmas
of the Alpine night, where the great pines stand motionless
waiting for fairy-tale characters to move among them:
nor the Christmas of the old cities
with their windy squares of lovely twisted houses
where the boom of the cloud-solid cathedral bells
spreads over everything like a new colour:
nor even the Christmas of the great renewal
the tiny fingers of the Redeemer clutching a stalk of straw
and the patient animals stamping or moving their ears
dropping their harmless dung in the font of the world's birth
on the barn floor where time starts again: none of these things
came to my mind when happiness said *Christmas:*
but a town Christmas, entirely of this world
full of the kind of materialism that brings happiness.

I thought of a large and well-heated house
with people standing about on good carpets
continually going up and down stairs, and ringing for taxis
as each new homing person arrives at the station
and the thick winter air outside, embalming the house
with its double-glazing and mince pies, and lights
switched on in every room. And I thought of children
going to bed too excited to sleep, and whispering
and giggling, and going to sleep at last
in clean safe beds, and the grown-ups
standing on chairs to reach down the hidden presents
bought in November and carried home through fog:

I thought of the taxis arriving, and the unwinding of scarves
and last-minute deliveries of things like sherry and chestnuts
and boxes of shiny crackers: yes, boxes of all kinds
especially those small elegant boxes for watches or rings
very carefully swaddled in clean white tissue paper
far more of it than anyone really needs
and tied with that hard black ribbon that curls up like metal.

And I thought of their opposites, very large parcels indeed
and people undoing them greedily and happily
and throwing the paper down on the floor in great rustling nests
and everyone's eyes bright with acquisitiveness
and selfish well-being, but also with gentleness:
and through the middle of everyone, like the flame in one of those
hundred-hour candles, love of themselves and of one another
yes, love, shining so plainly through walls of coloured wax.

JOHN WAIN

THE REUNION

1

you will never forget this.
you are poised at the
        center of the salt
white landscape, grainy &
        blurred in your white shirt
your thin wife beside you in
        her clean dress, your son run
off, every daughter pregnant

& sullen in the heat. each of you
        stands on his own
long shadow facing the horizon
the dark

cows blowing & twitching on the
        yellow sky. nothing
happens. the dead air burns
        in your mouth
like metal, tomatoes swell
on the vine.

2

the table trembles on its
locked legs. still
        they do not come.
*will they think
        our lives empty, will we
have enough:* warm rye
loaves, the last of the hens
sour pickles, milk in the stone

jug. the plowed fields
settle & drift,
the face in the dark
　　shine of the wood is
not your own.

3

at last the black
cars come
　　bumping over the furrows.
stiff pigs start & scatter
your hands begin to shake you
　　stab out for your wife she
is not there she is
　　kneeling under the table
praying for rain. you know they

are bringing in their black
　　baskets tiny jars full of your
own blood. they pull
up they do not get out your
　　daughters begin to wail
you can see diamonds glittering
　　all over them like
small flames at the throat &
　　in the hair. when

they open the doors & step
　　out their eyes are like
all the ice in your dreams
& each pale
　　mouth you bend
to kiss falls open, smelling
of vinegar & lined with glass.

DAVID WALKER

VARIATIONS ON ECCLESIASTES

For everything under the sun, a time, a reason.
Coffee and toast at breakfast,
Christ's body for my dinner once a week,
Cocktails or wine at 5:00 o'clock,
And the dark sweetness of your body when in season.

Time for the secular city and a time for prayer,
A time to open doors, a time to lock,
A time for picket lines, a time for writing verse,
A time to lay you down in darkness
To be the ground bass to the singing air.

I never say a prayer before I love you.
I offer simple human strength and weakness.
I think that God commends our privacy.
Or if God's dead, my back will bear the bleakness
Of cold nothing. You have me above you.

CHAD WALSH

WORDS, FOR A DEAD GEOGRAPHER

Tonight he is funeral-parlored, among his friends;
Tomorrow will have let himself down
In this forsook ground, not home, not
The Isis, by Iffley, at evening,
Where late he summered. Lover of maps,
A man tender to place-names,
Tonight he goes chartless, goes hatless,
Somewhere through territories whose guidebooks do not exist;
And what vehicles carry him follow no roads,
To no ends, save in heart's geography.
The memory of him ought not to fix to a rock
In a strange churchyard, but be cairned in stones
By an English wayside, at the fork of green lanes,
Himself to be known as a place-name.
He was at home in his learning,
Perhaps is at home still. Words only
We can give you, friend, and in your cold hand
This cartograph of the stars to steady your course.

NANCY G. WESTERFIELD

THE WRITER

In her room at the prow of the house
Where light breaks, and the windows are tossed with linden,
My daughter is writing a story.

I pause in the stairwell, hearing
From her shut door a commotion of typewriter-keys
Like a chain hauled over a gunwale.

Young as she is, the stuff
Of her life is a great cargo, and some of it heavy:
I wish her a lucky passage.

But now it is she who pauses,
As if to reject my thought and its easy figure.
A stillness greatens, in which

The whole house seems to be thinking,
And then she is at it again with a bunched clamor
Of strokes, and again is silent.

I remember the dazed starling
Which was trapped in that very room, two years ago;
How we stole in, lifted a sash

And retreated, not to affright it;
And how for a helpless hour, through the crack of the door,
We watched the sleek, wild, dark

And iridescent creature
Batter against the brilliance, drop like a glove
To the hard floor, or the desk-top,

And wait then, humped and bloody,
For the wits to try it again; and how our spirits
Rose when, suddenly sure,

It lifted off from a chair-back,
Beating a smooth course for the right window
And clearing the sill of the world.

It is always a matter, my darling,
Of life or death, as I had forgotten. I wish
What I wished you before, but harder.

RICHARD WILBUR

FALLS COUNTRY

for Peter Skryznecki

I had an aunt and an uncle
brought up on the Eastern Fall.
They spoke the tongue of the falls-country,
sidelong, reluctant as leaves.
Trees were their thoughts:
peppermint-gum, black-sally,
white tea-tree hung over creeks,
rustle of bracken.
They spoke evasively,
listened to evident silence,
ran out on people.

She hid in her paintings,
clothed, clouded in leaves;
and her piano
scattered glittering notes
of rain in sunlight,
drummed with winter storms,
opened green depths like gullies.

He took better to horses—
the galloping sound of hoofs
like eucalypts chattering
or stones hopping on slopes.
Enclosed in the dust of mobs
or swinging and propping
among those ribbony boles
he was happy.
His eyes were as wary,
as soft as a kangaroo's.

Snow falling, the soft drizzle
of easterly weather
covers them, my old darlings.

What does the earth say?
Nothing sharp-edged.
Its gossip of lichen and leaf
its age-curved granites
its glitter of wetness
enclosed them.

Is the spring coming?
Are there hooded orchids?
That's what their bones breed
under the talk of magpies.

Listen. Listen,
latecomer to my land,
sharer in what I know,
eater of wild manna:
      there is
      there was
      a country
that spoke the language of leaves.

JUDITH WRIGHT